# Rainbow in the Stone

## Robert A. Neimeyer

MERCURY
PRINT • DIGITAL • FULFILLMENT

A CONSOLIDATED GRAPHICS COMPANY

# Rainbow in the Stone

## Contents

## I SING TO THE EARTH

## COMING THROUGH

## ARS POETICA

# Foreword

Mostly, poetry is a private art with public aspirations. As a consequence, it benefits from the right mix of solitude and community, of moments of delicately held attention to inward or outward landscapes, followed by the audacious attempt to capture features of what is discerned in words that are intelligible to responsive others. My own writing is certainly given shape by this dialectic. It often finds its impetus in a meditation on the human drama — my own or that of others — or in singular observations arising in moments of contact with the larger world of which we are a part. But poetry does not begin to gel from such encounters until words — just the right ones — take form in a way that might spark something in an imagined reader, and ultimately, most poets hope, in actual ones as well!

The poems that comprise this collection, all written between 2004 and 2006, benefited from this blend of solitude made possible by my patient family, Kathy, Eric and Michael, and also from the responsive readings of fellow poets, both professional and amateur. In the former category, I especially appreciate John Bensko's laser-eyed precision in identifying the unneeded tissue that contributes to a poem's weight, but not its muscle, and Mary Leader's encouraging ability to take pleasure in the voice of what she termed "a modest prophet." In the latter group I feel particular gratitude to my friend and fellow dreamer, Bill Tuberville, my spiritual "brother," Alex Tyree, and especially my most reliable muse, Claire McGoff, whose ability to indwell the work of another has improved many of the poems to follow. And finally, I appreciate the gift of your readership, opening the hope that words written in silence might yet speak to another.

*Robert A. Neimeyer*
*September, 2006*

# Lessons of Loss

## In Summer

In summer there are days like these—
untended hours, fallow.
Like a bare patch of earth they clear space
for something—a volunteer tree, perhaps,
or crabgrass like we had in Florida.

That's the problem with time:
it seeks nothing, accepts anything,
lets events pile up like accidents.

And so we, who are addicted to order,
must impose it, be the curators
of the past, file our lives,
bind them tight into sheaves of days.

Looking at my bookshelves
I see this is my one, true profession—
to catalogue time, conserve the moments.
This is why I have tucked the CCC hat
behind the German field glasses
just above *The Outline of History*,

set the amber bottle of Tussonex,
its label typed by my father's hand,
next to the Darkie Toothpaste, its minstrel
icon beaming scandalously.

This is the secret reason
that the Hopi kachinas find a place
near Joseph Campbell, dance around
the actual skulls of small animals

who gave up their spirits in my woods
in a bid for immortality.

This is the hidden order in the shadowbox
made of a typesetter's tray hung on my wall,
my high school ring, my mother's glass dogs,
a robin's egg, a plaster Indian
safe in the slots.

All of these things huddle close to the books,
the type.  They are trying to become words,
to make their way into sentences.
Mute nouns, I thread them with plots,
swaddle them with themes,
give them a place in this story world.

But at the end of a long summer's day
as I shift toward sleep,
I know that the covers of the books
will not swing wide like open doors
to these unpublished things
when I turn out the light.

Instead, night will begin
to reclaim this home,
silence these stories,

clear a space

that will lie fallow
until a new day comes.

## What Morning Brings

What morning brings
is different each day,
and the same:
A call to rise up
from the depths
like a fish circling,
circling,
toward the light
that dissolves our dreams,
the only world that is fully ours.

And so every day
begins with loss,
and compensation—
the long splash of sun
across the floor,
the first cool walk
with the dog,
the trees nodding
in greeting.

Soon enough we will all go
our separate ways, but now,
for a moment we linger,
stretch into the same room
of day, yawn,
rub yesterday from our eyes

to make way for something new.

## *Drift*

The sea sloughs off its dead
like a scouring hand,
its shores an ossuary for
countless lives.  Their frail husks
splinter underfoot, reduce to
something elemental.
Their soft bodies yield
to the hunger of passing gulls.

It is to this strand we drift
to shed our shells,
bare our flesh for the cleansing.
Like sandpipers,
we wade into the waves,
retreat before their power.
Ambivalent as flotsam,
we ebb and flow,
seek the balance of holding
and releasing,
until spent,
we press our heavy shapes
into the scree of shore,
and its fragile forms
into our own.

## Drink

*See*, she said, *your father* —
stumbling, spilling himself
into the orange stain of chair.
Like nervous birds,
we watched from the stair
as the darkness
took him, held us fixed
in the light of her anger,
the curl of her spiteful lip.

     Released,
we fled to our separate cells,
to our dreams fed by fear,
the sudden crash
of lamp to floor.  We awoke
to full bladders,
empty stomachs,
teeming brains,
too cowed to risk the walk

through no-man's land.
The hulking black Packard
out the window
confirmed his presence,
the tire's track in grass
a sign of warning,
like a serpent's path
at water's edge.

It took years for the drink
to pull him under,
lift him above
the terror of his dimming sight.
In the end, the weight
that bore him down
was too great for children's arms.

When the cold stone of his grief
slipped free of care,
we staggered under shifted weight,
moved forward from the trap —
        granted freedom
by the sudden
amputation.

## The Others

They mostly come at night,
robed in darkness,
ask why we left,
where we've been.
They do not so much want us back
as to remind us
of what we have
lost, could not embrace
in the confines
of our singular lives.

We dare not look them
in the eyes, the moonlit pools,
drawing us in, and down.
We step back to firmer ground,
reach for our anchor,
sense its weight.

Worse is when they come
not for us, but for our partner,
make the easy error
of slipping into our dreams instead.
They cut through our resolve
with their thin lips, razor smiles.
They freeze us with their gaze
as they step lightly toward the door
with their dancing shoes

to answer the whispered bidding
of a more intimate call.

## What the Body Wants

Around and within
this rigid cage of bone,
the flesh pulses with desire.

What it wants is obscure,
indecipherable as tea leaves,
the runes of a lost race.
Even at rest, each muscle
in its salty heaviness
throbs with unfinished

action:  a halting step,
a choking swallow,
a breath
        arrested.

Only the heart keeps beating,
beating, like a vagabond knocking
on door after door, to be turned away
unfed.

What the body seeks to find
is loss
of boundaries in ecstatic merger
with another being,
complementary in its insufficiency.
Or else the sweet oblivion
of sleep, or death,
cool and leaden with
        nothingness,

its dark hairs reaching
into every cell
to find the secret
of its atomic tick
and turn it

off.

## In Age

They resist the graying
that comes with the weathering,
the denial of color,
the bleaching of years.
They don red hats, plaid shirts,
restore the falling plumage.

They hold fast to things gained
with the spending of time—
a spoon from Silver Springs,
a yellowed letter from camp,
photographs of the dead.
They are the custodians of memory,
of regret.
In the evening, they heave
the sigh of release
from the weight of too much knowing,
recline in bodies burdened by hope.

They fumble in their pockets, in their purses,
with the decisions left to them,
worn smooth as old tokens.
They wait, uncertain
as browning roses,
for bright night
to awaken and
explain
a life.

## Siege

It began with the forgetting,
the betrayal of words once loyal
to the tongue and ear.  Then,
like a spreading rebellion
of the inanimate,
the uprising was joined
by eyeglasses
      slippers
            dentures
                  keys,
all fled to base camps
at the jungle's creeping edge.
By the time familiar faces
resigned their names,

donned masks of anonymity,
the battle was lost—
a rear-guard action
to cover day's swift retreat.

As night advanced
the self's stronghold
fell to the incessant siege—
the gaping holes
      where once mirrors hung
revealed the woman in the wall,

the terror in her eyes
the last bridge to give way.

## Stationary

I grow weary of this world,
its shroud of obligations
pulling me down to earth like gravity.

I want to stand still,
motionless,
grow small and quiet,
until this coarse robe falls away
like a spent chrysalis
after the transformation.

Now there is only waiting —
the uneven tick of time,
the rustle of dry flesh,
brown leaves resistant to a freeing wind.

The broken threads of speech
lose hold on restless ears,
and emptiness fills the air
like a sudden cloud of doves.

In the light of forgotten colors
I scan the parchment of my life.
Whose hand was it that wrote those words?
and for what imagined reader
did the lines take shape,
composing themselves into
consecutive life sentences,
duly served, coming to rest,
like a pendulum's
slow descent
into silence?

## Cleaning Fish

Her perpendicular eye finds my own.
　　　*End this*, it says,
in a liquid language silent as the sea.

I wield the knife
like the swift gift of the shark.

My woman's hands,
burned dry by the chemo,
move as if attached to other arms.
The left, assured, clasps her trembling form.
The right, uncertain,
opens her white flesh,
marbled through with crimson strands.

The eggs I remove, the scales I work free.
　　　She is readied for the pan.

Pink ribbons, like her veins,
thread through our family line,
link the soft bodies of my mother,
　　　my sister,
　　　　　myself —
Weedy wombs, overfull, become
lagoons for the kelpy strands.

Few but the dying know
the peace of resignation.
With surgical precision, we
excise the unneeded tissue from life,
scrape clean the arteries of purpose,
the nerves of electric connection.

Emptied of ambitions,
we are hollowed mouths
opened to cup the flowing water —

caught fish on a stringer
pegged tight at shore's edge.

## The Life Aquatic

The place to sleep
is in the bow of a boat,
far forward, below deck,
almost at the water line.

There, at the precise intersection
of two worlds, you will be held
in the soft arms of the lake or sea,
feel the rocking, rhythmic,
repeating the beating of your heart,
the pulsing of your blood.

Only yesterday in night's dark cradle
I became a fetus in his mother's body,
as she was strolling, or making love,
lulled by the hollow amniotic thunking
of the waves upon the hull.

It is a deep liquid instinct
locked in every cell
that convinces me that we evolved
from something aquatic,
crawled reluctant onto land,
lost our way back.

Of all the ways that we can die,
drowning would not be the worst,
slipping under again,
like a flying fish,
into the primal medium
after a brief plunge into sun.

It must come as relief
to drop our ridiculous insistence
on puffing out words
with small breaths,
to let go the fraught quest
for bipedal balance
on the rocky earth.

I imagine that last great release
of air, like a galaxy of silver planets
rising toward the light,
a final salute to gravity's slow pull.

And I can sense the sinking,
dropping down into the deep,
certain affection of the water,
enclosing me like a womb,
inviting a reverse ontogeny,
my cells joining, rather than dividing,
simplifying in geometric regression
toward a unity

before the separation began.

## Bond

When my mother gave up her flesh
like a threadbare coat,
she spread into the room
as a vapor fills a closed space.
      Gradually,
she permeated us,
our sponge-like bodies
her needed shelter.

She fills us now
as we once filled her,
animate, moving, electric
with quiet potential.
The birth she seeks
is in memory, thought,
the dedicated act—
the ways spirit finds form.
All that we are points back
      to her,
as the branch retraced
finds trunk, or root.

What will become of her
when the rags of our bodies
fall away, and we too reach
for the haven of lives not our own?

Will a part of her, dilute
as weak tea, accompany us
in the outpouring of our souls?

Or will she find freedom from flesh,
as the cicada abandons its hard husk
to seek a final home in the air,

and release from bondage
to love?

## Visitor

Mother, it's been four years
and still you come,
reaching with your ghost-arms
for one last embrace.
Your heart flutters like a canary
in its rusted cage of ribs,
looking for a latch
it never found in life.

Endlessly patient,
you never demand,
never push in where unwanted,
never draw attention to yourself.
Demure, you wait in the wings,
nod from the window of a passing train.
You watch over my shoulder in a game of cards,
making your *tch tch* sounds
when I discard the Queen of Hearts too soon.

Sometimes you come in conversation,
smiling at the time-burnished image
of you with fishing gear,
small and pert as a cat,
ready for one more cast
as your children's heads fill
with a misty blend of stars and sea.

You save your sad eyes
for the private moments
or the sisterly whisper, sibilant
with loyal grief.

Mostly, you come at night,
wrapped in the dark paper
of a dream, rustling
like yesterday's newspaper.
In day, you hang in the air like cigarette smoke
burning the eye, wafting in blurred curls
as thin as your body,
and as sharp.

You have found a way to speak
with no words, in sepia tones,
a pilgrim in your own small home.

You, you sit at your solitaire table,
or vanish, vulnerable in your double bed,
half-vacant for 40 years,
married still to my father's ghost.
And me, I stand alongside
with an empty plastic bottle from Lourdes
in the shape of a battered Virgin,
with none of Bernadette's healing water
for your parched lips.

They say the skull grins in perpetuity,
but yours never does,
your wan, brave smile
more haunting than Mona Lisa's,
more binding than Marley's chains.
And chains you wore,
links forged of hard, cold memory,
riveted cuff shackled to your frail bones.

Now, for me, you are that hard memory,
that urge to revise,
an unfinished poem
that yearns for a triumphant coda
to make sense of the whole.

In its little boy love,
an unsleeping part of me
will stop at nothing to mend your life.
Its wet and reaching fingers trace their tearful path
from your face to my own.

## To Brad, in Quietude

How strange it is now to address you,
in the quiet of an evening like we never shared.
Then, the brass boom of your baritone
banished all doubts,
like the horn of a tugboat
knifes through fog.

Now, I speak to you in your absence,
your only reply the measured tick of time,
as its tape of seconds
marks the distance from an unmet goal.

Still we wonder:
How could doctor's hands,
intent on saving life,
stop up a life so large?

And how could your great gasp,
eager as a newborn's drawing air,
elude the fluorescent gaze
of those who knew to watch?

You gave up your self the way you
built it, by degrees,
like  an onion spoiling from the outside in.
In the end there was the marriage of machines:
The metronomic pulse of stubborn heart
paired with technologic lung,
its hollow thrum more sure than death.

Then round your bed,
like animated drones around a dying queen,
we huddled, swarmed, and left
      as we felt the axis shift.

# *Vigil*

*For MADD Canada, committed to stopping impaired driving and to supporting the victims of this violent crime.*

We came here to find
what we had lost.

*Margaret Lawlor, April 14, 1937-February 6, 1996*

From the Maritimes, before the thirst
of summer brings more death.
From BC, whose sunsets spill the blood of day
on seas indifferent to desire.
From Alberta, whose endless roads
continue their black work.

*Marie Therese Monette, September 4, 1983-January 1, 2002*

People of hardy stock,
accents flat as the prairie.
Francophones, voices accented by need.
Immigrants, traces of homeland
clinging to their consonants,
their vowels,
like dried earth to the treads of boots.

*Waclaw Piltzer, August 18, 1951-June 20, 1981*

Voiceless,
none asked to join this caste,
each nominated by a random hand
unsteady on the wheel.

*Angela Stephens & Jason Skells, June 1, 1987/May 1, 1987-May 14, 2004*

The docile ghosts
find their places on the board.
They stare out at the ardent
with their prom eyes,
their wedding smiles,
expressions of fossilized hope.

In black and white or fading colors
they mingle, lounging
in their easy chairs,
      their living rooms,
          their cribs.

*Raymond Mitchell, December 15, 1997 (unborn)*

In unison, they greet us
with their quiet countenance,
patient as dried flowers.
Like Vonnegut's Pilgrim,
they have become unstuck in time.

*Priya Vaidyanathan, July 19, 1971-June 28, 1992*

So too it is for those of us who set the shrine.
Left standing at the dance,
before the altar,
in the nursery,
we keep faith with the lost.

*Bobby Amero, July 8, 1977-May 12, 1984*

We seek the thin consolation of stories
well rehearsed, echoed in the hollow
of lives too like our own.
Tonight we join in blended grief,
anger lighting the two hundred candles
that are shorter than our memory.

## Reading Sandburg

There is not so much distance
between Ypres and Mosel,
between Verdun and Baghdad.

The poet's spade still digs
beneath the grass,
its steel-blue edge sharpened
on the grindstone of bones.
His narrowed eye traces
the exposed roots,
the cheapening of lives
in power's blunt exchange.

Sands too, like time,
cover all.

## Bare Bones

We are the bones,
relics of spent lives.
We bleach in the sun,
endure in urns and crypts,
know the repose of a closed hole.
We shed honor
like autumn fruit
falling on packed soil.
The living move on.
The dead have no memory.

The living move on.
The dead have no memory.
The earth is our ossuary,
our tomb of forgetting.
We have become strange
to the ways of continuity,
the grief born of transition.
Stripped clean of the flesh
of connection, we accept
your indifference
        with indifference,
the grace that comes with anonymity.

We are the bones,
and the dead have no memory.

## *Stone Tears*

You steer toward the harbor of our talk
as a ship pushes through fog,
the hope of safe passage, a beacon;
the cargo heavy in your hold.

Your eyes carry your grief
like stone tears,
their swell too sudden to restrain,
too weighty to let fall.

To release them would cost you
 all that remains
         of connection.

Like ballast,
the dead weight of your loss
balances, restrains,
holds you to measured meter.
With it, you move
slow as the tide,
ebbing and flowing
with your own rhythms.

I watch your approach
as I stand on shores lapped
by these same waves.  Like you,
I found this uncharted coast
in the black vessel
of mourning,
my only service now
to stand
         and wait.

# Bendígame*

*Spanish — petition for a blessing

*For the chaplains of the Rio Grande valley,*
*to whose work this is a footnote*

The forty voices rise as one
in morning prayer.
They sing the old songs,
worn smooth as burnished coins.
The copper faces are *centavos*
that have crossed the river
to find their worth.
In the light of benediction
they glow bright as gold.

I was brought to this valley
to teach the wise of death,
recite theories like *milagros*
of lesser force.
It is enough.
At the table to the side
an old woman folds back the years.
Her tears find the furrows
that lead to her breast:
the grave of her infant son.
Like rain in the desert,
they water the flower of her grief.

In the dim light their eyes meet mine,
reaching as an open hand, their ears
a bridge across the borders
        of our lives.

A pale ghost,
I am the echo of the dead.

In their buried wisdom
they teach us how to mourn.

## There is a World

There is a world
that knows no grief,
a world beyond human design.
The silent pines and enduring rock
of this shoreline
are only where they are.
They long for nothing,
regret nothing,
aging unconsciously in the tidal slurp
before giving themselves
back to the sea and earth.

Unlike the rooted trees
and stolid rock,
we have no place,
only the hollow consolation
of errant mobility.
Self-conscious, we yearn
for that we do not have,
forsaking the loyalty of familiar attachments,
for the ephemeral enthusiasms
of that which cannot be.

And so, unknown to ourselves,
we quicken to the erratic pulse
of ambition and desire,
setting the fishhook,
then tearing it free,
from the flesh of this,
our only world.

## Prayer

May all that which my life raised up —
these works, these loves —
hold firm a time beyond my passing.
May they nourish other lives
as others nourished mine,
give scope for new beginnings.

And in the end,
when the music of my life
fades in the earth like an echo,
may all those who held me
in their words or arms
let me pass
       into them,
              through them,

and fall back among the living.

## Solstice

In winter's chill the year draws down,
the day's light muted as a veiled face.
Now the early night comes for us,
claims our waning hopes,
our unfulfilled dreams,
all that is left of ambition.

This shadowed cleft stands between seasons
like a valley between mountains —
a dark passage toward dawning light.
The low slant of sunrise dissolves
unmet goals, unreached destinations,
makes room for the hope
that comes with forgetting.

The year's division
marks our lives, cleaves them
into chapters of waning and waxing.
We conform to it as we do to breathing,
a cycle of releasing
        and reopening,
seeking the beginnings
made possible by completion.

# I Sing to the Earth

## Petroglyphs

There is a grace
in going free of talk,
swimming upstream
toward the source of words.
Before its birth,
all speech grew ripe in silence.

It was in that time
that sense sought stone,
that hands red as the rock
scraped patina from the cliff.
They found the shape of deer,
of snake,
sacred in their primal light.

They told the way
of coming and going,
traced the great circle
and the four known winds.
Gods too ancient for a living name
moved these hands
to define their form.

Now, the canyon murmurs their chant,
a wind of words just beneath hearing.
The old hands with their tongues of flint
have long grown still,
turned to dust.
They have entrusted their ways
to the walls of rock
that lock tight their secrets
like an echo in the stone.

## Utah Triptych

### 1. *Climbing down*

The blaze of morning
ignites the cliffs,
evaporates the moon,
hanging ghostly as the coyote's howl.

It is time to begin the walk,
to be swallowed deep in the throat of rock,
time to climb down,
beneath history,
through the saline memory
of ancient seas
washing the earth
like a scouring hand.

Now the sea rises hot within us,
spills out,
seeks sand, sky,
the root of Utah juniper,
the cone of piñon pine.

It falls away
like a tear of lament.
It bleeds back
into the raised ribs of earth,
glowing yellow as bleached bones.

An old ache throbs still
beneath the pulse of words.
It pulls us
toward the vacancy of arches
fixing us with their empty stares.

The sun leans into us,
and we lean into the rocks.
Each footstep carries us
deeper into earth,
deeper into sky.

Like the desert,
we ripen toward subsistence.

## 2. *Raven's roost*

We thread through
the sand, the scree, the slickrock,
like shallow roots.
The land's emptiness seeps into us
with the ochre dust.

Like sentinels,
the great columns of stone
witness our coming,
our going,
impassive as the lizard's stare.
Life here withholds its secrets
from the unblinking eye of sun.

We stop to allow our words
    to catch up with us,
receive the gift of shade
poured from the upturned bowl of rock.

From a crevice above,
a fragment of nothingness dislodges itself,
shrieks down on us
on a storm of wings.

The raven, its iridescence black as loss,
reclaims the harbor of night
in day's dead heat.
A dark animus,
it shadows our steps
as we depart,
harbinger of a midnight
that is not yet ours.

3.  *Escalante*

From the plains of rust red rock
the bluffs rise up,
verdant as an evening song.

The aspens and pines
have gathered the silence
and held it for our ears.
The woods fills our eyes
with the knowledge of green.
The desert is a shadow
we have forgotten.

Everything here is an act of creation.
Even the deer merely confirm
the presumption of life.

Like the stream that feeds
and bleeds the escarpment,
we pass through, and down,
to find an arid ground
to ease the letting go.

## Fire Ring

She toiled all day
for this harvest of rocks,
pulled like reluctant teeth
from the red gum of earth.
Now they ring the pit,
wearing their clay stain
like a low growl.

An ancient voice taught her
to shape this hole,
its stony symmetry
an echo of timeless chants.

Others of the tribe have laid the trail.
It is an ochre snake
winding down to the shallow pit,
open as a ready mouth.

With cloak of dusk
drawn tight over blue green hills,
the elder crouches
and ignites the brittle wood.
With small cracks,
like a nut giving up its fruit,
the sun's flame
unwinds from the logs.

Slowly they gather,
drawn to the circle
of the pit's orange glow.

Unneeded language burns away
like spent kindling,
opening the silence between words.

Then the stories awaken.
Grey ghosts curl skyward with the smoke,
climb the dark ladder of night
toward the place of the ancestors,
alive with stars.

Idylls of the clan
teach the young who they have been.
They mark boundaries in time,
word glyphs,
embers of history pulsing
like a tribal heart.

In dawn's soft light
the youngest rises to tend the coals,
coax life from quiet ash.
Soon, a father's hand
scatters sacred seeds and resin
among the lapping flames,
and with them fresh promise
of renewal of the rite.

### *There was a Time*

There was a time
when the siren songs of cities called to me
in their nocturnal luminescence,
offering the illusion of perpetual day.
Night's allure was limited
to the clandestine draw
of minor vices made more venal
by the midday sun.

Now, Night whispers more softly,
beckoning gently with her dark hand.

> *Come aside*, she says,
> *See the pallid forms of trees in moonlight,*
> *quiet sentries of the kingdom of the wood.*
> *Hear the chorus of small beings*
> *joyfully proclaiming their invisibility,*
> *as they shed their daily cloak of silence.*

I walk amid the ghostlike forms,
adding the crunch of boot on earth
to night's symphonic hum.
And in this womb of soft reflected light,
I discern outlines of inner forms
washed out in light of day. I stop,
and like the night,
invite small voices to have their say.

## For This Moment

For this moment
the crickets and frogs are winning
the battle of the bands.

No hush of night, this —
but a wild cacophony of calls
that muffles the distant drone of cars,
like a blanket pulled up over head
on a chilly night.

Oh, the evidence of human hegemony
is clear enough, even here —
the sturdy architecture of these buildings,
the very chair in which I sit.

But nature, insistent and perennial
even in this autumn wood,
murmurs rhythmically,
*We are here, we are here.*

## The Old Home

When we bought this old home
we opened its white clapboard box
as poor children unwrap a Christmas gift —
incredulous, timid, as if
there were some mistake.

Inside we found rooms emptied
of lives, the ghosts swept out
with all their  possessions.
Still the curling gingham wallpaper
sung "nursery," the floral print with its faux brocade
insinuated "lady's bath," the clawed doors
scratched out, "lonely dog."  Archeologists,
we scraped back layers of living like flaking paint.

In the thicket in the back we found
remnants of the chicken coop
beneath the twisted love of vines and wire.
We discovered chunks of coal, anthracite-black,
hardened as the laborers who once
shivered round the stove, tilled these fields,
picked the fruit to ship to privileged homes.

Even now, 15 years later, the past keeps leaking in.
This week, transplanting azaleas,
Jose pointed to a rusted steel flange,
biting up through the soil like a broken tooth.
*Peligroso*, he said, *dangerous*,
and I knew he was right.

I took a few shovelfuls of earth
and covered it,

weary of the weight
of too much history.

## The New Tree

It shook the night
as close thunder
in the wind.
The wood broke loose
like the rending of dreams,
a limb leaden
with spent purpose.
All that followed
was the protest of small branches,
ineffectual as a drowning hand.

As if resurrected,
the sundered limb defied
our morning search.
No furrow in the ground
marked its collapse,
a scattering of leafy shroud
the only token of its fall.

Irony dawned more slowly
          than the day.
Where yesterday
only grass sought sun,
the limb now stood,
thrust into the earth
like a cutting
to be made whole
and to be
reborn.

## 8 o'clock

and still black as midnight
the cars coursing
two, and two
on this river of asphalt
wet with morning
mist

Lights of stores
punctuate the night
with their yellow ovals
their red lightening
their neon shouts

And in the parking lot the cars
aligned as teeth
cast grey dry shadows
on the pavement
huddled round

## Stream Beds

The hills rise up
from the river's edge,
frustrate the geometry
of the farms.

From the main artery
the veins fan out,
serpentine creases
where no water flows.
Like neural convolutions
they are the memory of the land,
engrave what came before.

Where has the water gone?
There is the answer:
to holding ponds
unnatural in their roundness.
It flows through
silver capillaries,
straight and hard as purpose,
center pivots,
mobile rivers
to wash out the intolerable
uncertainty of seasons.

Like ambition,
the fields yield
no hostages to time.

## Edge of Time

From this high perch
carried skyward by its own design,
the black disk of yesterday
slides away into oblivion.

And at the world's sharp edge,
impossible in its scope and clarity,
a thin chromatic fire announces
        birth of day.

Gradually, almost beneath perception,
a crimson blade splits
the two fixed spheres,
and dark eternity gives virgin birth to time.

The same incandescent moment
gives rise to sky and sea.
Mottled purple now sculpts the sleeping earth,
an indigo cloak hugging tight to fading dreams.

Above the great divide of light
day's spectrum slowly spreads.
Intense tribunal hues
bleed away to pale pastels.

Too soon, in the gaze of rising sun,
Earth takes familiar form:
Common clouds and hackneyed sky
crowd out audacious dawn.

As the cleavage of timeless night
diffuses in measured hours,
I wonder:
Is there anything more sad
than an act of creation
betrayed by its own fecundity?

## Conquistador

Today I stand at the spot
where, in 1528, Cabeza de Vaca stood
with the remnants of his *conquistadores*,
their clothes hanging like tattered sails.
This haven — *Bahia de la Cruz* —
was the portal to a New World,
he wrote in his *Narrativas*,
sent as an extended postcard to Spain.

I wondered what possessed him, then,
this man with the head of a cow,
to set out in a fleet of improvised boats
into the immeasurable Gulf,
spending down the few lives
left in his purse for the passage.

Perhaps history spared him
in his hard quest for Mexico
as it needed his quill
to sketch the blueprints of these
high-rise condos, thrusting up
like ambition from the manicured curbs.
Perhaps it required his force of will
to break ground for the pilings
of the endless causeways, laying
claim on these islands as fences pen
a wandering herd.

As I gaze at the stilled waters
in their concrete grooves,
he looks back with a vacant stare
at the palms and sculpted hedges
that corral these lives,

and dons a smile of bovine
satisfaction.

## El Mezcal

The familiar restaurant greets
the *gringo* who leaves the worn shoes
of his language at the door,
enfolds him like a woven rug.

In the light of simple interest
a young waitress beams, claims
her roots in Sonoran sand,
speaks feeling with the words.
        Drawn back
by a string of sentences,
the curtain of roles opens,
reveals a culture's treasure
like Aztec gold.

In the week since I last came
the waiters have discarded
the anonymity of thin white shirts,
donned crisp new garments —
substantial, tailored, and tan
as their skin.  This simple act
done in solidarity has lifted them
above servitude, joined them
in a higher order —
the embroidered insignia
with its *saguaro* script,
a badge of pride.

And for one chameleon moment,
long and cool as a desert night,
I imagine I too can shed my whiteness
like an old skin,
take on new color,
and find a place on their flag.

## Mariza

Song made flesh,
you light the night with your eyes,
their flash the pulse of summer lightening.
Trees sway in your hum,
await the coming storm.

The *fado* breaks from you
like a sudden gale.
In the swelling waves of your voice
the sea rises like passion,
falls hard upon the shore.

Siren of sadness,
you draw us in, submerge us
in your longing,
the anguish of a too-known world.
You fill us without resistance,
carry us sodden into silence,
your raised brow a hook,
the flicker of your smile a lure.

Helpless,
we open to you
as fish relinquish their endless night
for one short pull into day,
for one long shiver of feeling.

## Why Does the Sea Come to Me?

Why does the sea
come to me,
reaching with her feathery fingers
toward my perch
on these obdurate rocks?

With measured meters each wave laps
at this resistant shore,
a salty tongue
extending and withdrawing,
tasting the flavors of the stone.

What does the sea
say to me,
murmuring like a restless crowd pressing
insistent against constraining fence of land?

A rhythmic rumble,
broken by the shout of wave on rock,
an indecipherable idiom
commanding the attention
of a foreign ear.

But who am I
to sit upon this granite throne,
seeking meaning in the mumbles
of the sea?

An accidental presence,
a vagrant muse—
no part of the timeless talk
of surf and stone—

whose hubris hopes to hold
the liquid loquacity of this place
in the cupped and fragile hands
of words.

## Old Naval Guns

They stand at attention along the shore,
like outcroppings of vessels sunken
beneath the waves of sand.

The *cañones* of Cochrane, Pratt,
that carved this continent along its spine,
separated it surgically by force of arms.
The rusting turrets of *el dictador's* destroyers,
power welded tight to paranoia.
      Stubborn as the rocks,
the long grey line salutes the Chilean flag.

Now they guard only the gathering silence,
the forlorn beach, the occasional lovers
whispering passion into each other's mouths.

Inscrutable as the statues
of Easter Island, they have forgotten
who brought them to this place,
and why.

They have turned their backs on the city,
given themselves over to time,
its sandpaper working, working,
to rub out the echo
of their roar.

## Poem on the Back of a Bookmark

It's the *piazza* that calls it forth,
this trapezoidal square
colored in *Antique White* and *Burnt Sienna*
like a box of Crayolas.

Only poetry is needed to complete
this scene, catch it on a postcard
for others who cannot hear
the Italian flowing like the fountain
from the mouths of nymphs.

But if verse could shore up
the sagging cathedral, restore
the fragments of arches,
it would be done,
the products stacked in racks
at every corner store.

Instead the winged lion of *San Marco*
fixes us in its stony gaze, stands outside
of time, beyond the reach
of poets' hands,
whose fingers peck out
words like nervous birds
on the tables of cafes.

## Cinque Terre

Only two weeks ago we labored
up the hill from Monterosso,
its flags of beach towels
waving goodbye in the breeze.

We hiked toward terraced vineyards
combed into the slopes,
their green sinews tangled
as wind-blown hair.

We watched the sun as the sun watched us,
saw it fall into the rocks,
rise again as flowers
tenacious as a beating heart.

All day long we followed that trail,
climbed slowly on the thermals
of seaside cliffs, above the azure glass
of ocean, translucent as an iris
on the orb of earth.

Then, answering gravity's hard tug,
we stepped down, and down,
into towns nestled in the cleft stone
as if they were scree
scoured from the surrounding slopes.

Each of the five towns left its own
impression on the rumpled coast,
as distinct as fingerprints,
and as alike.

Vernazza, drawing us deep
into its constrained basin of harbor,
boats floating like airships
above the sea's cupped palm.

Corniglia, its zig-zag stairs
lifting us 100 meters above the shore,
above the filament of rail
that pierces the mountains,
threads these towns like precious gems.

Manarola, where we strolled
among canvassed boats pulled high
into the street, like the first
amphibians claiming land.

Riomaggiore, seducing us
with its tamed walkway,
well-traveled as the way of love,
graffiti grasping a blurred memory.

We hold these images now
in the unsteady hands of words,
shuffle them like postcards
with their fading ink
whispering their universal message:

*Wish you were here.*

## Rainbow in the Stone

In eons too remote
for human words to reach,
a great volcanic voice
commanded that the sleeping earth
lift up
and thrust dark shoulders into sky.

And so these peaks were born.
The youngest wear their bridal veils of white,
proud maidens
who have married with the clouds.
Others, brooding and barren,
turn their backs on the entreaties
of the sky.
Indifferent to the warm caress of sun
and cool whispering of wind,
they bend back toward a deeper pulse
in earth's hot throbbing core.

In this elemental world of rock and snow,
life finds a meager hold.
Neither thorny scrub nor unpaved road
brings color to this land.

Instead, the living earth itself
paints the stony forms.
Great swaths of ochre, sienna, verdigris and rust
wash the slate-grey rock.
In rainbow tones the arcing shapes
speak louder than the sky.
*We know a time before your own*, they say,
*— a time when earth could dance.*

## Ode to Baltic Amber

Syrup of life,
tree-blood,
protecting the woody veins
of prehistoric giants,
you did your work,
your magic,
turning sunlight into gold.

In that primeval forest,
before clocks wound tight the time,
you ripened in possibility
inside ancestors to cypress, yew and cedar.
You oozed toward portals
carved by the carpentry of beetles,
the swift intervention of the birds,
the accidental apertures
opened by beasts seeking
the cruel advantage of survival.

Pushing through,
you first glimpsed the sun that sired you,
felt the maternal moistness
of a world that conceived you.
Then you loosed yourself
from the tight womb of wood
in which you took half-form.

There
you swelled like a tear
from the tree's shut eye.
You grew,
gaining the strength of weight and purpose,

patient, holding.
You knew only the dull ache of yearning,
the thick pull of gravity
wanting final rest.

Until,
in a leap of love and longing,
you pulled free,
perfect in your completeness.
You fell like resinous rain
upon the fertile soil.

No mere seed,
seeking fruition in its replication,
you were already all you needed,
a drop of light swallowed up
in darkest earth.

And there you hardened,
in the fullness of your being,
waiting,
more patient still,
for a remote future
to unearth your golden sun,
and let you warm the hearts of man.

## I Sing to the Earth

I sing to the earth
and she to me,
two voices,
one song, a harmony
of sound and silence.

I sing to her
of purpose and of pleasure,
the rhythmic beat of knowing
pursuing its ambitions,
the taste of love and olives
in a harvest of delight.

She sings to me
her long, low note of birthing,
rising from blue oceans,
from fields pregnant with beginning,
from the wombs of sentient beings
yearning to unfold.

I sing to her
my heaving sigh of longing,
from the well of need and giving,
calling for completion,
an echo seeking resonance
in a canyon not my own.

She sings to me
her lullaby of patience,
the song of bulbs of hope in winter,
of a season's frozen hardship,
of seeds planted and seeds scattered
that yield to promised warmth.

I sing to her
My keening song of grieving
for the loss of loves and living beings
whose hands once held my own,
for places and possessions
now laid to waste by time.

She sings to me
of the art of eager dying,
the quick burst of collision,
the broken husks of dreams,
the sweet relinquishment of holding
that readies for release.

And as I sing I listen
to the chorus of vying voices,
some rising and some falling,
waves swelling and waves breaking,
my own a brief companion
to earth's enduring song.

# Coming Through

# *Opening*

On the far side of your life
something calls out,
seeks union with what
it has not met.
Like the hollow of a bowl
it sculpts the shape
it must contain
in the form of its absence.
Without this fullness,
it is merely decorative,
       waiting.

Only in stillness
can you discern this void,
know the emptiness
as specific as your open mouth
or the chambers of your heart.
Only in cultivating receptiveness
like a cupped hand
can you let the world pass in
       and through,
and ready yourself
for the meeting.

## Norma's Kitchen

In a far corner of the farmhouse
across the living room, whose walls
are lined like a crate with panels of true oak,
the kitchen hums with women's work.

Husked corn roils on the blue flame.
Peeled potatoes dance with steel
to thinness for the fatty vat.
The white porcelain of tabletop
waves its flag of red
around the edge, draws
our hungry eyes to the feast
of apple pies, their crusts
standing like golden domes.

How many hours did I stand
on that linoleum floor,
looking up,
          then across,
                    then down
on the counters that surfaced that world?

Here I retreated
from the ritual slaughter of chickens
in the back yard pen, unprepared
for their headless rush toward death.

Here I came after cycling
down the dirt road with my cousin, Alana,
perched like a hood ornament
on the handle bars of her bike.

Here I ran for the oasis
of ice box with its silver hand
clicking open like a safe
guarding the friendly bottles of 7-Up—
*You like it, It likes you* —
worn rough and chipped from seasons
of diaspora and return.

I look back on that scene
through the inverted binoculars of forty years,
the image clear, but small, receding,
like the boy in that tableau.

# Building

This evening, in the theater,
the drama on the screen was heightened
by your slight frame beside me.
Then, you tracked the twisting plot undeterred
by the tangle of adult ambition,
the fallen debris of decaying dreams —
an Eagle Scout pursuing magnetic north.

Tonight, in Lego-land loyalty
to the simpler geometry of childhood,
you sit cross-legged on the carpet,
hug tight to your thirteen years.
You are an architect in plastic blocks
and primary hues.
      I, your father,
follow your example, and seek
a lower center of gravity.
Together, our fingers fan a rainbow pile
in search of shapes
to restore a tiny house unbuilt for seven years.

The album that you chose unwound the time.
*"Teach... your children well..."* and
*"Feed... them on your dreams...."*
Eyes meeting in the sudden mist, we blink,
      step back to surer ground,
and heed the advice:
each father — and son — to the other.

## Thrift Shop

It doesn't smell happy.
Crowded clothes have discarded
their aging bodies.
They seek the consolation
that comes with time.
Hope, like the stale smell of cigarettes,
clings to yesterday's shirts.

It is here my son comes for inspiration.
Sixteen, and joyfully rebellious,
he paces between the rusted racks,
an impressionist assembling a palette
to paint a brighter world.

Possibility flourishes best in contradiction.
The Technicolor leather jacket,
red fedora and orange shoes.
The French cuffs of my youth
now gold-green hollows
from which slender hands emerge,
adolescent fauns seeking new pastures.

Above a khaki army and denim navy,
he floats, hovers, flutters,
an erratic butterfly,
exuberant emissary from a more chromatic land.

Accomplices to his performance,
vintage garments don wrinkled smiles,
mischievous elders regressed to an age
when they too knew how to fly.

## Warp and Woof

Something about this summer
brings to mind a loom,
its shuttle weaving, darting,
connecting the strands.

Enmeshed,
we cannot see the pattern
that is emerging, until it is
      a long way back.

All we know are the colored threads,
the return of Rob and Jae
from the Cape,
a visit from a Norwegian friend.
And we sense the stretching,
the hard pull of other hands
on the unraveling skein
of our children's years.

We are not even sure that this tapestry
is ours,
      or theirs,
           or yours,
                inter
           woven,
      engaged,
given shape by one another's lives.

In the end,
we thank you for it, thank them,
thank all who give us
the gift of a strand
or two, woven in,
a lengthening fabric to caress,
enfold, clutch tight
when winter gathers round.

## Eastern Passage

A long day's journey to the East
will bring you to a place
your soul has always known.
Only in meeting those who abide
in this other world will you
know the way home.
Here there are no destinations,
only passages.

With crafted accents they will speak
to your heart, work it like jade
to bring forth its beauty.
Masters of trade,
they will make the exchange,
accepting your offerings,
bestowing their own.
Among them you will move as a friend,
receive the gift of trust.
Coming is enough to earn it.

Leaving,
you will travel heavy with the weight
of what you have left, borne up
by what you have found.

Home will be transformed
by the passage.

## Your Presence

Your image has been with me all day,
and it has kept me good company.
It hovers like an angel in the mist
of my thoughts, caressing
like a summer breeze.  It lingers
in the last light of day, a wisp
of cloud holding fast to setting sun.
It gentles me into night,
the echo of your voice
a hymn of celebration.

How is it that you can intensify my day
like the sudden song of birds,
their voices harbinger to dawn?
What lets you awaken a seed
buried long in the soil of my life,
send the hairs of its root
deeper to support the slow unwinding
of stem, pressing through,
leafing out to sun like the spreading
fingers of an opening hand?

It is too much to know.
In the end I accept your presence
as the grass accepts the dew,
with the unearned grace
that comes with miracles.

## True Work

Make ready to hear the call.

Behind the clamor for your attention
it will come, persistent
as gentle rain.

It will not command with the voice
of assignment or deadlines,
will not measure its pace
in calendar squares.

But it will be there,
steady as the breath beneath speaking,
        and as quiet.
Stillness is needed to hear it,
to find synchrony with its rhythms.

Each step in this direction
will suggest the next, and with it
the path will unfold.

The first movement is but the beginning.
The way will change
        as you change,

as it changes you.

## Coming Through

Fall silent and you will hear it growing,
insistent as grass through asphalt.
You know it has always been there,
pregnant with possibility, finding form.
Now it is coming through,
seeking light,
earning a visible place
in this world you have made.

Listen.
Like a known voice in a crowded room
it will come,
follow the silver thread
of attention to reach your ear.
It only requires attunement,
a paring away of excess
to hear the pure tone.

Like sculpting hands
you must work the substance
to find its essential form.
There is something inside the mass
for which your life is the template,
awaiting the accident of discovery.
Now you must caress its naked shape,
shiver at its frailty,
know its strength.

All you have been has readied you
for this becoming.

# Ars Poetica

## What Now

What now
needs to be written,
to claim a more solid place
in this world of words?
A muffled breath,
a thing apart,
        standing back,
inchoate as a building storm.

Can a need arise
without an object,
thought without image
or form?  Like a mold
awaiting wax, I open
        the space,

uncertain that the fill
will come.  No forcing
will make it happen,
        and no wait.
All that there is
is the sense,
and all that has sense

is mute.

## Feel the Space

Feel the space
from whence a poem comes —
a moonlit hollow,
a clearing in the wood,
opening to shadow-forms
of inner life.

With night-sharp eyes,
scan the contours of this world.

What just leapt up
to catch a fragile beam
before retreating to night's
silk-dark womb?

With liquid sureness
now the subtle shapes emerge,
stepping lightly toward
a silent siren call.

What web of words
as delicate as thought
can hold the fleeting forms
and pin them to the page?

## Why We Need Language

We need language
like we need a key,
to escape the confines
of a literal world
that clamps tight like the iron cage
of moments merely lived
and not known.

We need the lift of words
like birds need the air,
to transport us on the clouds of sense
above the dark stone
of earth and death
to glimpse the perilous purity
of the sun.

We need the fragile illusion
of continuity with ourselves —
the fiction of a past that was our own,
the audacious oracle
of a dreamy fruition
in a time unknown to the stars
or to the soft muscles of tongue and hand
that bring forth words.

## Befriending Words

Sometimes,
the words come quickly when called,
loyal friends responding
to the entreaty of an earnest voice.

Then,
they sense the need
beneath the hopeful call,
or know the moment of meeting
will ensure the visit's worth.

At other times,
they are reluctant guests
who yield only to the patient suasion
        of waiting.  They seek
a host who makes ready for them
through quiet inactivity,
holding out the silent invitation
of a partly open door.

Sometimes,
they will not come at all,
or assemble in small groups,
distrusting the uncertain fellowship
of words they have not met.

At such times, the Confucian host
will resist the easy satisfaction
of coerced encounters,
and allow the time
that cautious words demand.

# Flight of Words

*To Claire, for her responsive reading*

The words fly north, then south
in electronic migration,
their small flocks etched
on flat-screen sky.

They answer the call
of abundance,
travel to complete
the circle of their lives.

Alighting in the field
of her vision or mine,
they animate the space,
invite the attention
of a studied eye.
A memory older than their own
has learned to trust this place.

Soon, the wheel of time
will return them to the tree
where they were hatched —
their numbers thinned,
pruned to hardiness
by the flight.

## *The Poem Itself*

should be a living thing
earn voice
song
breathe the air of its rhythm

Beneath the words
flows the theme
languid
      muscular
           impatient
full in its potential

Vertebrate
structure wrapped
in verse
pulsing
veins of emotion
dilating
constricting
readying for
        release

Then:  movement!
Verse      lurches
moves steady
    erratic
as a hand over flesh
quickens
     massages
        tugs

transmits its aliveness

jolts the listening
eye
to a series of small
      leaps

## Authority to Know

This is the lie
that masquerades as art:
That we must speak only from
the accidental confines
of our lives,
our words the small coins
we have earned for our labors.

Who then will speak
for the earth, if not
those whose veins
carry the sea's silent surge,
whose flesh feels the force
of the land's hard hold?

Who if not those
whose eyes strain to see stars,
whose ears hear the murmur
of the dead in the rocks,
whose downy hairs rise
to meet the chill
as sunflowers lift their heads
to greet a new day?

We were born
to speak a world,
to grow meaning
like blackberries
to redeem the thorns.

Like fruit, our poetry
is the fusing of earth
and light,
    a taking up,
        a transmuting,
and a giving back.

It is our rootedness
in deeper ground,
in something that abides in us,
that grants us
the authority to know.